Socialism and Religion
The Socialist Party of Great Britain

Contents

PREFACE To The Second Edition

THE CALL for a new edition of this pamphlet so soon after its original issue is proof that its message is heeded and its frankness welcomed.

Its publication is a challenge. It meets those professed Socialists who claim that religion and Socialism are in harmony, and those rabid opponents who rave of the "Socialist menace" to religion, with a plain statement of the facts. The anti-Socialists, however, ignore the vital attack upon their whole position, and simply use some of its evidence against their pseudo-Socialist competitors. The latter, on the other hand, maintain a very significant silence on the subject. This attempted boycott, as futile as it is cowardly, is sufficiently explained by the logic of the position present in the following pages.

It was prophesied that the issue of an official manifesto showing the antagonism between Socialism and religion, would hinder propaganda and make harder the work of recruiting the toilers for Socialism. But no such result has followed. At a time when so-called working class organisation complain of apathy among the rank and file, or of a decrease in numbers, the Socialist Party has to record a greatly increased activity and a considerable accession of new members. This is only to be attributed to the logic of passing events and the all-round propaganda activity of the Party, but it shows that the statement of the truth regarding Socialism and religion by no means hinders the advance of the cause.

In the present pamphlet a vast subject has been compressed into a small space by the rigorous exclusion of non-essentials, and without, it is believed, any sacrifice of clearness. Moreover, the many quotations given serve not only to show the authoritative nature of the evidence, but also to indicate where further information may be obtained.

Many further illustrations of the truth of the contentions made in the body of the pamphlet have come to light since the issue of the first edition. But from a fear of overburdening the argument, we quote only the following Nonconformist boast of the commercial value of "missions to the heathen." It adds a fresh point to the position argued for in the pamphlet, that modern Christianity closely reflects capitalist interests. The President of the Assembly of the Baptist Union on Missionary Day, 1910, said:-

"...Labour given and money spent in foreign missions, regarded even in the most business-like way, were good investments.... The export trade of our country would be much smaller if foreign missionaries had not in days gone by opened up new countries by proclaiming the Gospel."

A "good investment," undoubtedly, as far as the capitalist and his churches are concerned, but from the point of view of the "poor heathen," how should we describe the transaction by which he has been brought to exchange his country and his liberty for a bottle of rum and a pair of trousers?

The Socialist case against religion differs widely from the usual Freethought position. There are Rational superstitions as well as Christian. Religion was not the wicked invention of charlatans, nor is the passing of superstition simply to be explained by the "triumph of Reason." As shown in the following pages the "march of mind," the development of science, and the decay of religion, are themselves ultimately explicable only from the evolution of economic conditions.

Ideas play a secondary part in social development. They are the effects of the material environment upon human beings, and are not the creative motive force of social evolution. Consequently, in his worship of the "idea" the bourgeois freethinker is, like the Christian, attributing miraculous powers to the figments of men's brains.

The fact that the attitude outlined in this pamphlet is an integral part of the Socialist view of life, guarantees that the religious question will not be allowed to overshadow the main issue. It indicates, indeed, that the necessary work of general Socialist education (which includes the position here laid down on religion, as the greater includes the less) will be unflinchingly continued. It is a work that has remained for the Socialist Party of Great Britain to consistently develop.

In this work of education we are glad to acknowledge the debt the toilers owe to Marx. It is fashionable in superficial labour circles to patronise his undoubted genius, while professing that his work is now superseded. By what? That is a question they cannot answer. Men who have obviously never studied his work repeat mechanically the twaddle of bourgeois apologists, and claim that they are "emancipated" from "systems" and from the "dogma" of Socialist principles. They take refuge in an inconsistent and lazy eclecticism, made up of odds and ends of bourgeois learning and a narrow rule-of-thumb expediency. It is as though the modern mechanical engineer sought to emancipate himself from the rigidity and "dogmatism" of mechanical science by going back to the pottering, rule-of-thumb methods of the garret worker! The impotent "freedom" of expediency is no compensation for the power given by comprehensive theoretic knowledge. The superficial expediency now prevalent in social study is, indeed, a confession of mental bankruptcy. Apart from looseness of thought, such an attitude often goes with a desire to curry favour with the powers that be, possibly with an eye to appointments. It is clear that the ruling class, on their part, cannot admit the truth of social science which demonstrates their uselessness and worse. They hide behind the "complexity" of social life, and refuse to admit the possibility of a science of history.

To suit their interests science must halt on the threshold of society; theory must be decried, scientific method derided, and its conclusions scorned in social affairs, because, forsooth, social science exposes them for the thieves they are! Their henchmen and camp followers, the "intellectuals," are ever ready to serve them. As an example: when the capitalist class was young, and its members directly concerned in the labour of production, it was "correct" to admit (with Ricardo) that labour is the source of value. As the capitalist became entirely an idle class, however, a less awkward principle became necessary, and the idea was accordingly propagated that not the producer, but the consumer, by his demand for goods, stated in terms of their utility to him, creates all values! The working class, who are painfully aware of the primary importance of their labour in all this, can scarcely take such phantasies seriously, and will fail to be convinced that labour is not the source of value until they find that banquets, palaces, and motor cars, descend on demand ready-made from the clouds.

It is because Marx has analysed the production of commodities and placed the labour theory of value upon a scientific basis, that he is anathema in capitalist circles. Hence capital's intellectual flunkeys vie with each other in attempts to find some plausible substitute for science in the social field. It is, indeed, amusing to note that hundreds of replies to Marx have been penned, and that every succeeding capitalist apologist, realising and confessing that all his predecessors had failed, essays once more the impossible task and adds yet another to the long list of testimonials to the impregnability of the Socialist position.

So with the Socialist key to history which has been applied in the following pages, and which we owe to Marx and Engels. It is of a piece with the analysis of capital. By it, as Engels says:-

"History for the first time was placed on its real foundation; the obvious fact hitherto totally neglected, that first of all men must eat, drink, have shelter and clothing, and therefore work, before they can struggle for supremacy, or devote themselves to politics, religion, philosophy, etc. – this fact at last found historical recognition."

But this also the ruling class cannot accept. As with the robber classes throughout history, they cannot admit that society in its advance depends, not upon their puny selves and their muddled ideas, but upon the daily activities of the mass of disinherited who produce society's means of existence. This fact only the social revolution can teach them.

Clearly, then, the science that is to help the workers in their struggle for supremacy can receive no help from the capitalists as a class. On the proletariat must its advance and defence depend. Theoretically as well as practically, the emancipation of the workers must be accomplished by the working class alone.

As part of the essential educational work that must be done before this emancipation can be achieved the present pamphlet has its place. It is an entirely proletarian product, and treats a serious subject seriously and scientifically. It is issued, not as the view of an individual, but as the accepted manifesto of the

Socialist Party on the subject; and agreement with it and the general position of the Party, entails upon every member of the working class the duty of joining the Socialist Party of Great Britain and helping forward its work.

THE EXECUTIVE COMMITTEE OF THE SOCIALIST PARTY OF GREAT BRITAIN.

January 1911.

THE SOCIALIST VIEW OF RELIGION

01 – THE NEED FOR FRANKNESS

Is Socialism antagonistic to religion? Can a Socialist be a Christian? These questions are repeatedly being asked, and are being answered in many different ways. Yet Socialism has an unequivocal answer to them, and it is the purpose of this brochure to make that plain. Unfortunately for the political trickster, however, that answer runs counter to popular prejudice – it will not win votes from those who are not Socialists – and therefore his tribe deprecate the free discussion of the implications of Socialism in regard to religion on the ground of "political expediency." It is urged that such discussion is unnecessary, and that it will retard the cause by prejudicing people against it. But it must be recognised that the policy of hiding the truth and avoiding discussion is precisely the most likely way to injure the cause. It is, indeed, a distinction of the Socialist Party that it stands for the fullest discussion of every point of its principles and policy. Moreover, since the Socialist view is right it can be shown to be so, and a knowledge of the facts will remove prejudice and help to arm the workers against hypocrisy and reaction.

An explanation of the Socialist position on this question is the more urgent now, because the hypocritical and time-serving procedure of so many professed Socialists has enabled those who are frankly our opponents to keep the anti-religion aspect of Socialism effectively to the fore. Politicians angling for votes and office, and organisations scheming for members and subscriptions, have almost all evaded the charge that Socialism implies atheism and materialism, either by pretending that religion is in no way related to the question of Socialism, or by asserting that Socialism is the outcome of religion, and is indeed, true Christianity!

No apology, then, is needed for the present pamphlet. A frank and definite exposition of the Socialist attitude is doubly necessary. And in the belief that the worker will be helped to see the hollowness of the charges of the anti-Socialist, and to avoid the pitfalls of quackery and confusion, the following summary of the facts is issued by the Socialist Party of Great Britain.

10

THE NATURAL HISTORY OF RELIGION

02 – THE GENESIS OF RELIGION

No idea of the relation of Socialism to the religious question can be correct that is not based upon an accurate conception of religion. This is of the first importance, for erroneous notions in this respect are responsible for much of the present confusion.

What, then is religion?

The answer to this question can be given most usefully and interestingly by historical analysis. "History," says the founder of scientific Socialism, "has been explained by religion long enough, let us explain religion by history."

The labours of many patient investigators – travellers, missionaries and ethnologists – have thrown a flood of light upon primitive religion, and, from the wealth of information they have provided, certain fundamental principles have been definitely established. It is generally accepted that the earliest form is that of ancestor worship, to which Herbert Spencer's Ghost Theory has given us the master-key; indeed, Grant Allen has shown, in his "Evolution of the idea of God," that what is called animism, or the accrediting of things, both living and non-living, with indwelling spirits, is but a side development of ancestor worship. Let us, then, briefly trace the rise of this early religion, confining ourselves to its main features.

The fundamental idea of religion is a belief in the persistence of life after death. Originally, and in essence throughout, religion is a belief in the existence of supernatural beings, and the observance of rites and ceremonies in order to avert their anger or gain their goodwill. "Corpse worship," as it has been tersely called, "is the protoplasm of religion." How did this arise? It is, of course, difficult for us to realise the mental attitude of primitive man. We live in immense communities, have access to vast literatures, and have inherited the results of the experience of many ages. In contrast with the savage, our command over Nature is of remarkable extent, and the advance of industry and science has substituted the idea of a regular natural order in place of a belief in the caprice of spirits. But the member of a petty tribal settlement was restricted to a very narrow circle of human intercourse, limited in speech, without industry, science, or literature, and all the accumulated knowledge of Nature's working that these have brought; and consequently the disquieting phenomena of death, loss of consciousness, hallucination, insanity, trance, and dream, together with the awful and seemingly capricious powers of the elements, presented a problem to primitive man that could not be correctly solved on the basis of his slender knowledge and experience. He read his own passions and motives into the elements about him, and thought he saw in Nature's working the activity of beings like himself. Moreover, his dreams were realities to him. He believed that the dead man he had dreamed of had really visited him, or that in his sleep he had really hunted in some distant forest – yet the savage had not left his companions, and the dead were still covered with earth. The idea of a ghost that could leave the body, was , therefore, irresistibly forced on him. The loss of consciousness of an injured man was to be explained by the temporary absence of the spirit from the body. Madness was possession by an alien spirit. The dead man, to the simple mind of the savage, still lived as a spirit, and might return. Fear therefore took possession of his mind; fear of the evil power of the dead and of their spirits in the trees, streams, and elements that surrounded him. This fear gave rise to religious observance.

Primitive man buried his dead, put heavy stones upon them or even drove stakes through their bodies to prevent their ghosts troubling the tribe; or he gave them their weapons and ornaments and made offerings of food and drink to them (even after the decay of the bodies had demonstrated the fact of death) in order either to appease the anger or gain the goodwill of their spirits. Thus in his ignorance of causality other than personal, the savage projected his own characteristics into the world about him and imagined its working as due to the activity of spirits, mainly malignant, who had to be conciliated or kept away.

From these early superstitious fears there also arose a belief in sorcery, miracles, and witchcraft. Herbert Spencer states that

"The primitive belief is that the ghosts of the dead, entering the bodies of the living, produce convulsive actions, insanity, disease and death; and, as this belief develops, these original supernatural agents conceived as causing such evils differentiate into supernatural agents of various kinds and powers ... Along with a belief in maleficent possession there goes a belief in beneficent possession, which is prayed for under the forms of supernatural strength, inspiration, or knowledge. Further, from the notion that if maleficent demons can enter they can be driven out, there results exorcism. And then there comes the idea that they may be otherwise controlled and may be called to aid; whence enchantments and miracles."

Thus religious legends of miracle, when adduced as proof of the divine origin of a religion, are actually evidence of its earthly origin and of its community with the crudest superstition of the lowest savage. Primitive man's knowledge and experience were not sufficiently extensive to give him the idea of an inviolable natural order. He believed that all things were swayed by the ghosts of the dead, and consequently the "miracle" was his explanation of a normal happening. So the whole of man's early religious beliefs were due to the limitations of his knowledge and experience. Religion, therefore, has a natural, not a supernatural, genesis.

03 – THE REFLEX OF TRIBAL LIFE

How completely religion was the outcome of material conditions may be gathered, not only from the character of the ideas connected with it, but also from the exactness with which it reflected the kinship and social forms of tribal society. Since the social world of primitive man was confined to his kinsmen, and these were his only friends, not only did the ghosts of his kinsmen loom largest in his eyes, but they also appeared to him as the least malignant or more friendly of the inhabitants of the spirit world, and more or less powerful in proportion to their importance during life. A great warrior kinsman thus, after his death, tended to become a chief object of tribal propitiation and worship. So gods began to be.

The burial-place of a great chief (often his abandoned hut) became the abode of a god to whom offerings were brought and before whom reverence was made. Thus the temple originated – it was originally a covered tomb, and retains that characteristic to this day. Tribal customs as applied to satisfying the supposed wants or appeasing the ire of the deceased became religious rites. And with the lapse of time and the flattery of his worshippers, the glorified personality and power of a great dead chief became magnified into the attributes of a great tribal god. At the same time his nearest of kin became naturally the mediators between him and the rest of the tribesmen. They became the keepers of the temple, the guardians of religious ceremonial, and consequently the early priesthood. Such are the broadest outlines of the origin of God, the temple, religious rites, and the priesthood. Herbert Spencer thus summarises the matter in the "Principles of Sociology."

"Awe of the ghost makes sacred the sheltering structure for the

tomb, and this grows into the temple; while the tomb itself becomes the altar. From provisions placed for the dead, now habitually, and now at fixed intervals, arise religious oblations, ordinary and extraordinary – daily and at festivals.
Immolations and mutilations at the grave pass into sacrifices and offerings of blood at the altar of the deity. Abstinence from food for the benefit of the ghost develops into fasting as a pious practice; and journeys to the grave with gifts become pilgrimages to the shrine. Praises of the dead and prayers to them grow into religious praises and prayers. And so every holy rite is derived from a funeral rite."

In another aspect also the dependence of religious ideas upon social conditions is clear. "Strangers" were not admitted to the privileges of tribal social life, or if admitted it was only in exceptional circumstances, and after an elaborate ceremonial of "adoption" into the tribe was gone through. This exclusiveness was plainly reflected in the religion of ancestor worship, for kinship with the dead ancestor was regarded as a privilege, and his intervention in mundane affairs at the request of his relatives was considered the prerogative of the tribesmen. A knowledge of the forms of worship that accumulated was, therefore, jealously kept from the "stranger." Disaster, indeed, was often attributed to the offering of "strange fire" upon the ancestral altar.

Moreover, the supreme importance of rigid custom to the tribe had a profound influence on religion. It is reflected in the careful preservation of religious ceremonial even today, and in the tenacity with which old and now meaningless forms are adhered to. In contrast to the constant change and hunt for novelty which characterises modern social life, the peaceful and prosperous continuance of tribal institutions depended on the faithful following of venerated custom. What was old was tried and safe, what was new meant strife and confusion. Innovation was a crime, and was punished accordingly. (Modern religion preserves this spirit, just as it perpetuates the mummeries of ancient society.) With the development of the religious idea, ancient and mysterious custom began to merge into "law" by becoming attributed to the glorified ancestor or god. So god became the lawgiver," and tribal custom became divine ordinance, while social bonds were undoubtedly strengthened. This phase is illustrated in the Old Testament, which, indeed, is valuable as an illustration of the later and transitional forms of ancestor worship; and much of it portrays clearly the religion and customs of a people living in what Lewis Morgan, the great American ethnologist, defines as the "upper status of barbarism."

As a belief, therefore, religion was the outcome of man's ignorance of Nature's working, and of the mastery which awful and uncomprehended natural forces had over him, while as rites and ceremonies it reflected the forms, customs, and unchanging nature of primitive society. Thus the obscurity of material conditions is the source of religion; God did not create man, man created God in his own image.

By the "inertia of the mind," religion tends to persist, even through vast changes in the environment, in so far as it serves some interest and does not directly conflict with the new conditions. But in spite of this tendency to independent existence, religion has been modified continuously as the result of changing conditions and interests; while, notwithstanding repeated endeavours to adapt the ancient legends to modern requirements, its influence has waned. Nevertheless, in the degree that it survives, religion reacts upon society; it is the paralysing hand of the dead past upon the living present.

As we must, necessarily, within the limits of a pamphlet, deal with the main stream of development to the exclusion of relatively unimportant variations, let us follow the next great step in religious evolution, and we shall see that the change from tribal worship to universal propagandist creeds, such as Mohammedanism and Christianity, was also the result, not of revelation, but of material change.

04 – THE RISE OF CHRISTIANITY

The well disciplined legions and magnificent roads of the Roman Empire played a most important part in disrupting tribal religion and organisation throughout Western Europe; and in this they were ably seconded by the political genius of the Romans, as shown in the policy adopted towards the various tribal religions. Provincial gods were granted an honoured place within Roman temples, and so the military allegiance of the subject races to Rome was supplemented by their devotion to their ancestral deities. By this means the religious exclusiveness of the conquered peoples was determined, and the Empire bound more firmly together. How all this prepared the way for religious change is thus indicated by Gibbon:

"The Policy of the emperors and the Senate, as far as it concerned religion, was happily seconded by the reflections of the enlightened, and by the habits of the superstitious part of their subjects. The various modes of worship which prevailed in the Roman world were all considered by the people, as equally true; by the philosopher, as equally false; and by the magistrate, as equally useful. And this toleration produced not only mutual indulgence, but even religious concord ......A republic of gods of such opposite tempers and interests required, in every system, the moderating hand of a supreme magistrate, who, by the progress of knowledge and flattery, was gradually invested with the sublime perfections of an Eternal Parent and an Omnipotent monarch.... The Greek, the Roman, and the Barbarian, as they met before their respective altars, easily persuaded themselves that, under various names and with various ceremonies, they adored the same deities."

So the soil was prepared, and narrow, exclusive tribal religion began to give place to universal propagandist religions which were more in harmony with the needs of the aggressive and expanding political State. Of these religions Christianity was one. It was not manufactured, it grew. It took centuries to develop. Its rites, beliefs, and ceremonies were not inventions, they were legacies and adaptations from the old religions that it replaced. Christianity, indeed, is a cemetery of dead religions. The great legal codes of Rome were the codification of multitudinous tribal laws. So Christianity (though not at all definitely and consciously) was the systematisation and adaptation of ancient beliefs in accord with the new social principle. It had an impetus given it by a more directly economic factor. With the decay of the Roman Empire, owing to the utter exhaustion of the Italian provinces by a wholesale and ruthless system of agricultural slavery, and amid unparalleled political and physical disasters, despair fell upon all, and upon none more than the wretched slaves. Despair and disaster drove men to religion for consolation, while as Prof. Seeley, says: "the age was religious because it was an age of servitude." The hopelessness of this world encouraged an aspiration for a world to come, and this provided the motive and helped to determine the form of the religious revival.

The religion that rose to chief place amid such circumstances could only be the religion of the subject and the slave. So Christianity, with its cardinal ethic of submission, was pre-eminently suitable, and was a most useful ally to the despot who was struggling for the throne. Christianity, says Professor Seeley:

"Produced a complete change in the attitude of the people to the Emperor. It made their loyalty more intense, but confined it within definite limits. It strengthened in them the feeling of submissive reverence for government as such; it encouraged the disposition of the times to political passiveness .... Constantine, if he was influenced by a wise policy when he extended his patronage to the Church. By doing so he may be said to have purchased an indefeasible title by a charter."

Recognised by the State, the progress of Christianity became very rapid, and the Church assumed more clearly the monarchical tendencies that has been developing within it. Indeed, the spread of Christianity throughout Europe was largely due to its utility as an instrument of government in the hands of kings.

With the dissolution of the Roman Empire, Western Europe did not entirely relapse into barbarism, largely because of the profound influence of the traditions of Roman world-power. And the Bishop of Rome, by his position at the heart of this traditional empire, came to be looked upon as its spiritual head. His position, indeed, had become definitely monarchical within the Church, and the Lombard conquest threw the temporal rule of the little territory about Route into his hands, owing to the Roman Governor being kept distant at Ravenna by the invaders.

This establishment of the Christian Church as a temporal power, indissolubly associated with the traditions of Rome, had an enormous influence on the future of Christianity, for it caused it to be eagerly sought as ally by the Frankish aspirants to the throne of a revived Roman Empire. The greatest of these, Charlemagne, was, significantly enough, crowned in Rome by. the Pope on a Christmas Day, in solemn confirmation of his claim to the title of Emperor, and as Prof. Jenks says:

"In the name of Christianity Charles the Great rolled back the tide of Saracen invasion from the Pyrenees, and established the frontiers of Christendom."

In Saxon England also, the establishment of political society was closely followed by the replacing of the older tribal religious forms by Christianity. The rule of the King and his warrior band over the agricultural settlements of the tribes undermined patriarchalism and weakened its religious reflex. Consequently, the conversion of Ethelbert of Kent to Christianity was the signal for the conversion of England. The new religion spread from court to court in the Heptarchy, aiding the kingship in its struggle with the older system of kinship, and introducing a model of political organisation that was the ripened result of Roman political experience. Indeed, the early days of the State show clearly the close connection between Christianity and the institution of monarchy, although the Church and the King strove in turn for mastery. As Prof. Jenks says in his "Short History. of Politics":

"Christianity well repaid the favour of princes. Under the cry of 'one church and one king', the older tribal divisions were ultimately wiped out, and England became one nation, with Church and.state in intimate alliance. Even more obviously had Mohammedanism the result of breaking down tribal divisions and establishing mighty kingdoms, like the kingdom of Akbar in India, the kingdom of Ismail in Persia, and the kingdom of Mahomet at Constantinople... The intimate connection between the King and the Church was the best possible safeguard against any revival of patriarchalism in connection with ancestor worship."

Thus the spread of "universal" religions was the consequence and accompaniment of the development of a new social system. Kinship ceased to be the social bond; its place was taken by an expanding military or feudal power. The older religion ceased to be in harmony with the social order, it gave place to a religion whose principle was not exclusiveness, but universality; and the ethic associated with the new religion was necessarily that of submission, in order to encourage the obedience to government that was essential to the security. of the political State.

05 – THE REFORMATION

From its origin in the early political or feudal State the unreformed Roman Catholic Church remained the religious counterpart of the feudal system as this developed to completeness. The "Universal" Church, indeed, became a great feudal power, owning one-third of the land of Christendom. But economic forces began to undermine feudal society; the social organism was developing to the point where it had to burst its feudal bonds; and those directly dependent upon the newer economic forces found their religious reflex of the real world correspondingly modified. It is not a mere coincidence that (as Professor Thorold Rogers puts it)

"The success of a religious movement has generally, if not invariably, been associated with a movement for improving the moral and secular advantages of those whom it seeks to benefit."

And religious movements have also often been in part the forms taken by racial or international strife. The Lutheranism of the German princes at the Reformation was largely their standard of revolt against the foreign rule of the "very catholic" emperor, Charles V, and rebellion against an alien yoke or interference has everywhere been reflected in religious matters. More important still, however, has been the direct influence of economic change upon religious development.

The Reformation in England is a type. It was the accompaniment of the revolt of peasant, yeoman, craftsman, and merchant against feudalism; and the Puritan rebellion was the culmination of this religio-political movement. The reason for this is not far to seek. In a scientific age the theoretic basis and sanction of great movements are sought in science, but in a theological age, when tradition holds overwhelming sway over men's minds, the theories that support and codify social and political demands are often cast in a religious mould. The smaller the circle of knowledge the greater is the influence of faith, and the more necessary does its sanction appear to those engaged in new and little understood movements. Moreover, those who found feudal institutions inimical in mundane affairs found it easy to believe that in religious matters they were equally wrong; thus such doctrines as were not in accord with their secular aspirations were least likely to be accepted as true while religious traditions were strained and reinterpreted in order to sanctify the new demands.

The pre-Reformation Roman Church was, in doctrine and organisation, the oppressive reflex of feudal society, and consequently it lost ground along with the feudal lords. It was, indeed, the development of the economic factors of trade, industry, and capitalist farming that threw burgher and yeoman into conflict with the feudal class and led them to question in the world of religion all that they found incompatible with their advance in secular matters. As their real social world had changed, its religious reflex had to follow. Economic evolution was undermining tradition and making ancient custom a broken reed; while the more extensive reliance on reason than on tradition that was directly. fostered by the new conditions, and the increasingly apparent necessity of going to the roots of things for knowledge, led men to question priestly authority and to seek religious truth in (what was believed to be its source) the Bible. And into the texts of the Scriptures, the Puritan learned to read the ideas of mental independence and democracy that were developing in him. But since the spirit of liberty and revolt could not easily be read into the New

Testament – the essentially Christian part of the Bible –
recourse was had to Habakkuk and Isaiah, for, as Professor
Seeley says:

"Passive obedience was plausibly preached by the Anglican
clergy out of the New Testament. When the opposite party
sought scriptural sanction for their principles of freedom, they
were swayed irresistibly back upon the Old Testament, where
rebellions and tyrannicides may be found similar to those
which fill classical history."

As the Puritan movement itself shows, however, religious
views were not without a powerful reflex action on mundane
affairs. The Bible had been distributed broadcast in the struggle
against the Pope; and reverence for its traditions, added to the
almost complete lack of other popular literature, gave it
prominence that can hardly be exaggerated. It became,
therefore, the alphabet of the Puritans, it coloured their speech
and distorted their politics, at the same time that it provided the
then inevitable religious sanction for their social and political
aims.

We find. indeed that Puritanism was weak in the industrially
backward North and West of England, and strong in the East
and South, where economic development had proceeded
furthest. The boroughs were the natural centres of its
enthusiasm, and the aspect of the Christian religion that was
favoured indicated in general the group of material interests
that lay behind. Modern Nonconformity, moreover, is clearly a
modified survival of Puritanism, and is also still the religion of
the small manufacturer, the shop-keeper, and small capitalists
generally; while its intense political activity reflects the modern
and reactionary phase of their struggle.

Much might be written regarding the economic basis of

Protestantism in all its phases, but it is sufficient here to lay stress on the fundamental part played throughout by the change in material aims and interests engendered by the development of the new methods of gaining the material living.

Say Marx and Engels:

"When people speak of ideas that revolutionise society they do but express the fact that within the old society the elements of a new one have been created, and that the dissolution of the old ideas keeps ever pace with the dissolution of the old conditions of existence.

"When the ancient world was in its last throes, the ancient religions were overcome by Christianity. When Christian ideas succumbed in the eighteenth century to rationalist ideas, feudal society fought its death battle with the then revolutionary bourgeoisie. The ideas of religious liberty and freedom of conscience merely gave expression to the sway of free competition within the domain of knowledge."

Therefore, instead of the vast social and political changes that accompanied the great Protestant movements being caused by the new religious ideas, these ideas are themselves only explicable as the outcome of the rise of capitalist farming, industry, and commerce, and the advance of a new class to political domination.

06 – THE EXODUS OF RELIGION

In the light of the foregoing historical facts it is clear that religion has evoked continuously under the pressure of natural causes. and in this it does not differ from all other things; but a distinct characteristic is exhibited by religion's modern phase. In contrast with science, which grows in volume, complexity, interdependence, and definiteness, religion decreases in volume, cohesion, and definiteness, and is now in process of evolution – if such it can truly. be called – into nothingness. It is, in fact, more accurately an evaporation than an evolution.

From the dawn of civilisation, indeed, religious change has always been more remarkable for what was abandoned, rather than for what was added or retained. From being inextricably bound up with the whole social life of a people, it becomes a more and more insignificant reflex of the remaining dark corners of that social life. This is illustrated in the passing of its dogmas and beliefs. The vividness of hell-fire and the unending terrors of eternal damnation are considered mere allegories by many a modern Christian; and his views on miracles, the casting out of devils, and the creation of the world, would have been the cause of an auto-da-fe if adopted a few centuries ago. This fading of religious beliefs is unmistakably due to the accumulation of experience and the advance of industry and science, for these have shown that Nature is not moved by the caprice of spirits, but works according to an ascertainable and regular order. It gives point, moreover, to the truth uttered by Naquet that "whenever knowledge takes a step forward God takes a step backward." Fundamentally, indeed, the supernatural is totally excluded from the whole universe by the logical modern concept of an interminable warp and woof of cause and effect.

The present is rightly called an age of religious indifference, and religious censuses, such as that instituted some years ago by the Daily News, have made it particularly noticeable how largely this indifference has gained the urban proletariat. It is the development of industrial forces, and mankind's consequent growing control over Nature and increasing knowledge of her working, that provide a wider and firmer basis for science and leave less room for superstition in the minds of working men. Science itself is the direct outcome of economic development. It is the torch, which, as its flame is fed by material advance, sheds a light of increasing power and drives obscurity and superstition from an ever larger circle.

This indifference of the workers is fostered by the fact that religion, when put to the test, is ever found on the side of their oppressors. It is encouraged by the workers' daily contact with the hard mechanical realities of life which leave little room for illusion. In spite of their lack of learning, the mass of the toilers find no basis for belief in divine interference, and little reason for doubting that the inevitable sequence that we call cause and effect, as seen in all industrial processes, extends unremittingly over the whole world. The workers learn in the factory, that the most awful natural forces are regular, explicable, and controllable; while the feeling of helplessness before the powers of Nature, and the incomprehensibility of these to man, recede before the lessons of man-made productive forces that rival Nature in their giant strength and rational complexity.

As Paul Lafargue says:

"The labour of the mechanical factory puts the wage-worker in touch with terrible natural forces unknown to the peasant, but instead of being mastered by them he controls them. The gigantic mechanism of iron and steel which fills the factory, which makes him move like an automaton, which sometimes clutches him, bruises him, mutilates him, does not engender in him a superstitious terror as the thunder does in the peasant, but leaves him unmoved, for he knows that the limbs of the mechanical monster were fashioned and moulded by his comrades, and that he has but to push a lever to set it in motion or stop it. The machine, in spite of its miraculous power and productiveness, has no mystery for him. The labourer in the electrical works, who has but to turn a crank on a dial to send miles of motive power to tramways or light the lamps of a city, has but to say, like the God of Genesis, 'Let there be light,' and there is light. Never sorcery more fantastic was imagined, yet for him this sorcery is a simple and natural thing. He would be greatly surprised if one were to come and tell him that a certain god might, if he chose, stop the machines and extinguish the lights when the electricity had been turned on; he would reply that this anarchistic god would be simply a misplaced gearing or a broken wire, and that it would be easy for him to seek and find this disturbing god. The practice of the modern factory teaches scientific determinism to the wage-worker, without it being necessary for him to pass through the theoretic study of the sciences."

Upon such foundation, therefore, religion cannot firmly stand. Nevertheless, so long as the anarchy of modern competitive society exists, the accompanying obscurity and confusion in social life will continue to shelter superstition. This point is illustrated in the following reference by Marx to the United States:

"When we see in the very country of complete political emancipation not only that religion exists, but retains its vigour, there is no need, I hope, for other proofs in order to show that the existence of religion is not incompatible with the full political maturity of the State. But if religion exists it is because of a defective social organisation, of which it is necessary to seek the cause in the very essence of the State."

Class domination is the essence of the modern State. It is based on competitive anarchy and parasitism – the evidences of a defective social organisation. It still leaves room for religion, because it maintains ignorance and confusion by its structure and contradictions and because religion is fostered as a handmaiden of class rule. Nevertheless, the growth of the social forces of production within modern society, and the better knowledge the workers obtain of their true relations to each other and to Nature, loosen the chains of ghost worship and mysticism from their limbs and lessen the power of religion as a political weapon in the hands of the ruling class, while they form, at the same time, the material and intellectual preparation for an intelligently organised society. The matter has been put in a nutshell by Marx in the chapter on "Commodities" in "Capital," volume 1:

"The religious reflex of the real world can, in any case, only then finally vanish, when the practical relations of everyday life offer to man none but perfectly intelligible and reasonable relations with regard to his fellow men and to nature.

"The life process of society, which is based on the process of material production, does not strip off its mystical veil until it is treated as production by freely associated men, and is consciously regulated by them in accordance with a settled plan.

"This, however, demands for society a certain material groundwork or set of conditions of existence which in their turn are the spontaneous product of a long and painful process of development. "

It is, therefore, a profound truth that Socialism is the natural enemy of religion. Through Socialism alone will the relations between men in society, and their relations to Nature, become reasonable, orderly, and completely intelligible, leaving no nook or cranny for superstition. The entry of Socialism is, consequently, the exodus of religion.

THE SOCIALIST PHILOSOPHY

07 – THE MATERIALIST EXPLANATION OF SOCIETY

Our brief outline of the natural history of religion has shown that Socialism, as a system of society, means the end of supernatural beliefs. But that is only half our present task. What is the relation of Socialism as a propagandist movement toward modern Christian teaching? Or, since general principles should here be first considered, is Socialism as a working philosophy also opposed to modern religious ideas?

In the first place, all religious teaching is directly opposed to the scientific materialism, or monism, which is an integral part of Socialist philosophy. As Dr. Shadwell said at the 1909 Church Congress at Swansea:

"The purely materialistic view on which Socialism is based is absolutely opposed to Christian teaching."

Socialism does not – as does Christianity – mock the wage-slave by telling him that he has a free will, and that environment does not count. It points out the overwhelming influence of environment on the individual, and insists that to remove the poverty, unhappiness, and degradation of the many, it is necessary to depose the few and change material conditions. Socialism relies on an alteration in political and economic conditions for human improvement. It attributes to capitalist exploitation, and the social conditions this engenders, the general poverty, crime, drunkenness, and degeneracy. Thus it is entirely antagonistic to the Christian teaching that not social change but a "new heart" is all that is required. In contrast with the Idealist metaphysics of the Churches, the Socialist movement is materialist in philosophy, object, and method. Let us look more closely at this.

Since Nature has been discovered to work according to ascertainable and inevitable order, society as part of Nature can be no exception. The Christian ideas of free will and supernatural interference therefore become absurd, and give way to determinism. Natural history has shown us that the struggle for the food supply is the fundamental principle of organic evolution, and this cannot halt on the threshold of human society. Just as the available quantity of the means of subsistence, and how and where this is obtainable, has determined and modified the structures of plants and animals, and settled their mode of life: so man, being a tool-using animal, has his social organisation and mode of life determined in the ultimate by an essentially similar process. In both cases it may be said that the "economic" is the basic factor, for the overwhelmingly important tools or instruments of production, which are, in effect, supplemental organs to the human body, are represented in the lower organism by the special adaptation of its parts to the quest for food. In essence, therefore, this factor is as truly the basis of social evolution as it is of what is generally called organic evolution. The mainspring of progress of all kinds is thus material, not ideal.

To endeavour to explain social or organic evolution by its ideal reflex is to reverse the natural order. "In the beginning was the thing." The evolution of the brain, the world of ideas, and all intellectual activity can only be explained by the preceding and accompanying material environment, for any other attempt at explanation postulates something uncaused, which is contrary to all scientific experience. Intellectual changes are made and stimulated by material change. That ideas have an important reflex action on social conditions in no way alters the fact that material conditions form the base, origin, and material of all intellectual life.

Obviously, in order that there may be ideas and human history, two material things must first be present: human beings, and food and shelter for them. And the fundamental fact that is so seldom realised is, that where, by what means, and how much, food and shelter can be obtained, determines if, where, and how, man shall live, and the forms his social institutions and ideas shall take.

It is, indeed, the very basis of Socialist philosophy that, in the words of Frederick Engels:

"In every historical epoch the prevailing mode of economic production and exchange, and the social organisation necessarily following from it, form the basis upon which is built up, and from which alone can be explained, the political and intellectual history of that epoch."

This materialist concept is the Socialist key to history. It has been applied in the preceding analysis of religious development. It is the first principle of a science of society, and, being directly antagonistic to all religious philosophy, it is destined to drive this "philosophy" and all its superstitions from their last ditch.

It is usually asserted by Christians that the regeneration of mankind must precede, and not follow, social amelioration. They, therefore, expect hell to breed angels. General Booth, for example, says:

"Socialists want to make the world a paradise without having a paradise people."

But the Socialist knows that a paradise people could only be born of paradise conditions. Unlike the Christian, he does not expect figs to grow on thistles.

Even among those Christians who nominally accept "Socialism" this cleavage in ideas is not less marked. Their "philosophy" inverts the natural order. Thus Dr. Clifford , like General Booth, says:

"You cannot remould society out of illiteracy, indiscipline, intemperance, and selfishness .... Men are not 'moralised' up to the point where a co-operative community is possible."

And so on. He urges the churches to provide the impossible in the way of "man building" amidst capitalist conditions. But this, as a general policy, is as futile as it would be to expect to pick ripe and beautiful fruit before the soil and the season were suitable to grow them. The Socialist knows that industrial evolution and working-class self-interest are inevitably preparing "the soil and the season" for that social change that alone can make possible the highest development of men and women. The rise of Socialist ideas is itself but the reflex of this economic evolution and class interest. But the contradiction in terms known as the Christian Socialist is inevitably antagonistic to working-class interests and the waging of the class struggle. His policy is the conciliation of classes, the fraternity of robber and robbed, not the end of classes. His avowed object, indeed, is usually to purge the Socialist movement of its materialism, and this, as we have seen, means to purge it of its Socialism and to divert it from its material aims to the fruitless chasing of spiritual Will-o-the-wisps. A Christian.Socialist is, in fact, an anti-Socialist.

Clearly, then, the basis of Socialist philosophy is utterly incompatible with religious ideas; indeed, the latter have been reduced to their logical absurdity in what is called "Christian Science." Moreover, the consistent Christian (if such exists) could only look upon the existing world as an essential part of God's plan, to be accounted for only through God, and modified at God's pleasure. He could only regard those who sought the explanation of social conditions in purely natural causes, and who also sought to take advantage of economic development in order to turn this vale of tears into a pleasant garden, as men who denied by their acts the very basis of his faith.

The concept of God as an explanation of the Universe is becoming entirely untenable in this age of scientific enquiry. The laws of the persistence of force and the indestructibility of matter, and the unending inter-play of cause and effect, make the attempt to trace the origin of things to an anthropomorphic God who had no cause, as futile as is the Oriental cosmology, which holds that the world rests on an elephant, and, as an afterthought, that the elephant stands on a tortoise.

The inflexible laws of the known universe cannot logically be held to cease where our immediate experience ends, to make way for an unscientific concept of an uncaused and creating being. The Creation idea is unsupported by evidence, and is in conflict with every scientific law. Socialism is consistent only with that monistic view which regards all phenomena as expressions of the underlying matter-force reality and as parts of the unity of Nature which interact according to inviolable laws. It is the application of science, the arch-enemy of religion, to human social relationships; and just as the basic principle of the philosophy of Socialism finds itself in conflict with religion, so does it, as a propagandist movement, find religion acting against it, as we shall show.

08 – THE MODERN PURPOSE OF RELIGION

In the early, days of the political State the role of Christianity was revolutionary; it helped to disrupt the ancient order. Today, in the dotage of the political State, its role is conservative and reactionary. In its birth and death it is the ally of the forces of oppression. It helped to break down the last vestiges of early communism, and it is utilised now as a bulwark against the higher communism to come. That Christianity, in its individualism, its false idealism, and its political connections, is utterly opposed to Socialism is recognised by the capitalist class itself most clearly; while priests of all denominations proclaim with emphasis that religion is the antidote par excellence to Socialist ideas.

Addressing a meeting at Grosvenor House in support of the "Bishop of London's Fund," on Tuesday, May 11th, 1909, under the presidency of the Duke of Devonshire, the Bishop of London quoted a statement made by a slum missionary and described how a whole family in Notting Dale existed on five shillings a week, earned by a boy, and out of that four shillings was paid in rent. He said:

"Can you expect that boy to believe in the goodness of God? Will he not want to know where God comes in? Under all circumstances I cannot regard the prospect as rosy. In forty years the Bishop of London's Fund has built two hundred and thirty churches, and I believe saved London from such a revolution as would astonish the world. If it were not for the influence of religion, perhaps the people of the East End would not take things so quietly as they sometimes do."

New churches for families starving on one shilling a week! For, after all, the Bishop did not appeal to his noble and wealthy hearers to remove hunger and poverty; the point of his appeal was the necessity, not of feeding the starvelings, but of keeping them quiet. Such is the service religion renders to the propertied class. And the Bishop's appeal was not in vain. Within a month Mr. Morrison, the city millionaire, left £10,000 to the Bishop of London's Fund; £10,000 to the Bishop of St. Alban's Fund; £10,000 to the East London Church Fund; and £10,000 to the Rochester Diocesan Society. Mingled with the millionaire's thoughts of death was his instinctive solicitude for the interests of his class, and, out of the amassed wealth he could no longer enjoy, a portion was earmarked for the purpose of keeping the victims of capitalism from revolting.

The Church of England, however, is by no means alone. The Roman Catholic Church recognises that it, also, has a similar mission. The Archbishop of Westminster, speaking before the Society of St Vincent de Paul, at Manchester, on September 19th, 1909, deplored

"The terrible cleavage between class and class, which unhappily existed in this country."

Here in England we were face to face with "terrible social difficulties," Dr. Bourne declared, and in order that the people should not be carried away by their sympathies into the adoption of Socialist principles, he advised the teaching of the Catholic Church as

"a real bulwark against those theories which are undoubtedly gaining ground in this country."

After the Lord Mayor's show comes the dustcart. The majesty and solemnity of the Roman Catholic Church is followed by the big drum and cornet of Salvationism. In a "foreword" to the annual report of the social work of the Salvation Army – written by Mr. Arnold White, under the title of "The Great Idea," the author expresses

"the conviction that in the Salvation Army we have a strong barrier against Godless Socialism."

The main reason for capitalists' liberality toward religions bodies is plain. They know that religion is incompatible with Socialism, and look upon it rightly as a working-class soporific; indeed as Marx said, "religion is the opium of the people." And it is thus the agent of class domination, not only because of its beliefs and organisation, but also, in spite of opinions to the contrary, by virtue of the ethics with which it is associated. The teaching of the Gospels, as we shall show, so far from supporting Socialism, is directly hostile to it.

09 – WAS JESUS A SOCIALIST ?

The mistaken view so largely held today, that the ethics connected with Christianity are the essence of that religion, makes it necessary to include this aspect of the matter in our survey. The truth that ethics and religion are separate things is obscured by the confusion that reigns in the Christian camp. Frankness was never the characteristic of the priestly cult, and in the strenuous endeavours of up-to-date reverends to retain some hold upon the minds of the people, there is hardly any length to which they will not go. Some who deny the inspiration of the Gospels and accept the conclusions of science still claim to be Christians because they admire the ethics associated with that religion. Grant Allen, however, has clearly, shown in his "Evolution of the Idea of God" that religion and ethics had distinct origins and that their association is relatively modem and by no means universal. As a matter of fact, the so-called ethics of the Bible are no monopoly of Christianity. They existed before Christ and abound in ancient philosophies; while other and older religions, such as Buddhism, are connected with an ethical code in some respects superior to that of the New Testament. Buddha died in the fifth century before Christ; and Mr. A. Lillie, in his "Buddha and Buddhism," shows that there is an almost absolute likeness between the moral lessons embodied in the teaching of Buddha and those of Christ, and suggests that the so-called ethics of Christianity have an Indian origin. Buddhism, moreover, is the one religion guiltless of coercion. Not only, therefore, are the ethics not the essence of the Christian religion but they, are only Christian by adoption.

The most absurd claim of all, however, is that Christ was a

Socialist. This is the last refuge of the confusionist and mystery-monger. Let us briefly examine this claim. It is made, for instance, by Dennis Hird in "Jesus, the Socialist," "Clarion Pamphlet, No. 46." In that somewhat hysterical publication patriarchal regulations are quoted from the Old Testament, and two quotations from the Acts are given in reference to the communal life in the early Church, as evidence that Christ was Socialist! Yet it is obvious that neither the primitive institutions of the Hebrews, nor the monasticism of the early Church, have any connection with Socialism. The democratic ownership and control of industry, by and for the wealth producers could not come to pass before the capitalist system had developed and the productive forces had become social in character, therefore Socialism was unthinkable, and its propaganda impossible, two thousand years ago. Christ's denunciation of wealth is not Socialism. "Sell that thou hast and give to the poor" was his advice to a rich man. This is not Socialism, but anarchism and social suicide, for the wholesale distribution of aims is a "remedy" more deadly than the disease. "Take no thought for the morrow" was his repeated anti-social advice, and the whole trend of his teaching was to despise worldly things for the sake of a reward in heaven. But Socialism, on the contrary, is the appreciation of the things of this world and the endeavour to make a paradise here.

The contrast between Socialism and Christian teaching is plain even where the Christian precept is otherwise admirable. Thus we are enjoined to love our neighbours as ourselves, and to do unto others as we would that others do unto us. But the Socialist has learnt that present vile economic conditions make such an ethic utterly impossible of general application today. Ruthless exploitation and the antagonism of aims and interests that this implies together with the cut-throat competitive struggle of each against all that capitalism engenders, cause men to prey upon one another, and make the Christian precept a mockery. It can only become possible of general practice when capitalism is abolished, when cooperation replaces competition as the basis of society, and when the interests of each cease to be antagonistic to those of others, because economic conditions have made the welfare of each at last identical with the welfare of all. Therefore the materialistic movement of Socialism will alone make possible what the dualistic ethic is utterly powerless to bring about, namely, the fulfilment of the golden rule in so far as it is of any value to the human race.

Another important antagonism between the so-called Christian ethic and Socialism is illustrated by the modern Christ – Leo Toistoi (1828-1910) -who bases his teaching upon the Sermon on the Mount. In that sermon we are told, "But I say unto you, that ye resist not evil: but whosoever shall smite thee on thy right cheek, turn to him the other also". This cardinal ethic of Christianity has been the ally of despotism and oppression everywhere, and Tolstoi in his insistence upon this doctrine has been the best friend of the bloody Czar and the worst enemy of the Russian peasant. Non-resistance to evil is, indeed, criminal. Socialism means resistance to evil and war on the oppressors, for the only hope of the toiling millions lies in the extermination of evil. But the Christian doctrine means submission – and slavery. So the asceticism, self-abnegation, and professed other-worldliness of Christian teaching, which regards this earth as a vale of tears and a painful preparation for a life in the clouds, is an ethic of slavish degradation, and when taught to the workers it admirably reflects the narrowest self-interest of the exploiting class. It is an ethic that runs counter to working-class interests at every point. It is the counterpart, not indeed of a communist, but of an individualist society. As an eminent Prelate said at the 1909 Church Congress at Swansea:

"Individuality is of the very essence of Christianity."

And Christianity, we may, add, is by, the same token the very antithesis of Socialism.

10 – SOCIALISM AND ETHICS

The fact that Christian ethics, as we have seen, reflect capitalist interests against the workers may perhaps be more truly stated by saying that the prevailing ethic tends to express what is lacking in the actual conduct of men, according to the views or interests of the ruling class. The difference is not great, but it helps to bring out the truth thal the very existence of a code of ethics, whether admirable or not, is evidence of defective social organization. It is proof that social conditions impel men and women to do things that are against the prevailing interest. There is, for example, no need for philosophy to demonstrate that when we are hungry we should eat, but where in society, owing to disorganization and class oppression, the interests of men are antagonized, and they are urged to do things against the prevailing interest or social need by stress of environment, the dominant class impose their wishes upon the many in the form of ethics or moral instruction which the many are to adopt irrespective of their own interests. Where, on the other hand, the common good is visible and definite, and the interests of each do not conflict with, but promote, the interests of all, ethical codes as at present understood die out, for the plain pursuit of each individual's interest results in rendering all moral preaching superfluous by advancing simultaneously the welfare of the whole. This truth has been glimpsed by Herbert Spencer (1820-1903), for, in his "Data of Ethics" (p.243), he says:

"Here it remains to be shown that a kindred conciliation has been, and is, taking place between the interests of each citizen and the interest of citizens at large; tending ever towards a state in which the two become merged into one, and in which the feelings answering to them respectively fall into complete concord."

Moreover, the removal of confusion and the harmonising of the material interests of each with those of all, tend to make all activity which promotes social good, automatic or instinctive. For, as Spencer further says, (ibid,p.250):

"From the laws of life it must be concluded that unceasing social discipline will so mould human nature, that eventually sympathetic pleasures will be spontaneouslv pursued to the fullest extent advantageous to each and all."

Hence we are concerned, not with moral ideals but with material conditions, not with ethics but with Socialism; for to be obsessed with the need for ethical codes is to be the dupe of capitalist ideas. Ethics, even when honest, are but attempts to reconcile the irreconcilable antagonisms of capitalist society, and are doomed to sterility. With the abolition of class antagonisms the attempt to reconcile them becomes superfluous, and so ethics disappear.

So long as we have capitalist society, however, we shall have capitalist ethics imposed upon us, whether coloured by religion or plain as secular moral instruction or "ethical science."

Plain or coloured their object is the same; but it is not for naught that the ruling class are so eager for the religious moral instruction of school-children, for the effect is more marked in that form. The sophistication of the children's brains with superstition and hypocritical capitalist codes prevents millions from ever understanding their position in the world. Only when the influence of religion has been so weakened by social advance that it ceases to be useful as an instrument of government will the master class institute purely secular instruction. The poison will nevertheless continue to be administered. The religion known as patriotism, with its superstitions, its miraculous lying legends, its symbols, music, vestments, pomp, and ceremony, is even today more useful than Christianity, as a means of stupefying the workers and will continue to be used. And the slavish code which the capitalist class desire to impose upon the toilers will be perpetuated under the name of "moral instruction." The ethical societies, having divorced the class ethic from the supernatural, assiduously show the way, inculcating the falsehood that society is the reflex of the idea, misrepresenting materialism, and inverting the real order of things. Instead of impatience under robbery, resistance to oppression, and the class struggle for a better life which the Socialist recognizes as virtues, the propertied class insist upon patience under exploitation, submission, veneration of the institutions of robbery, meekness before the oppressor, and love for those who grind the faces of the poor, as the "virtues" they require in the lower orders.

An ethic, indeed, can be no more than a class ethic, because society is divided into antagonistic classes. The interests of wage-earners and profit mongers are opposed in the fundamental factors of material living, and the aims of one class are distinct from those of the other. The pressing need is therefore not ethics, but an end to the categories of wage-slave and capitalist.

"Morality is the result, not the cause, of social amelioration."

says Professor Jenks, and the battle for Socialism must usher in the peaceful and humane life of tomorrow. The worker's guide today must be no capitalist code, but the class struggle; and this entails loyalty and cooperation between members of the working class, and implacable hostility to capitalism and those who uphold it.

11 – QUACKERY AND CONFUSION

Since Socialism and religion are, as we have seen, irreconcilably opposed to each other, it may be both interesting and useful to note here the curious public pronouncements of so-called spokesmen of the working class on this question. They, will at least illustrate the existing confusion and show the need of plain speaking.

Mr. J. Ramsay MacDonald, M.P., in his book "Socialism" (Jacks),p. 101, says:

"Socialism has no more to do with a man's religion than it has with the colour of his hair. Socialism deals with secular things, not with ultimate beliefs."

But he also says in the same volume, page 99, that the Socialist "finds in the ethics of the Gospels a marvellous support for his economic and political proposals."

Mr. Chas. D. Drysdale, of the Independent Labour Party, in a pamphlet entitled "Socialism and Irreligion," sold through the I.L.P. Publication Department, says, crushingly:

"The most crushing reply, therefore, that can be given to the literary prostitutes who have reduced misrepresentation to a science and lying to a fine art, in the columns of the gutter press in their campaign against Socialism, is that the accomplishment of the Socialist ideal and the institution of the Socialist Order, instead of tending to the negation of theological religion, will have the effect of freeing theology from the shackles of present-day materialism, and of raising human ideas of the Supreme Being and the Infinite Beyond from the abyss of ignorant credulity into the realm of the

Intellectual and the Rational."

On the other hand, Mr E. Belfort Bax, in his "Essays in Socialism," says:

"The saying of Tridon, subsequentlv repeated by Bebel and others, to the effect that Socialism stands for a system of life and thought expressing itself in economics as Communism, in Politics as republicanism, and in Religion as Atheism, embodies in a few words a large measure of truth.

"It may be convenient for Socialists with a view to election expediency to seek to confine the definition of Socialism to the economic issue, abstracted from all the other issues of life and conduct."

And, significantly, enough, the Social -Democratic Party, (of which Mr. Bax is a prominent member) carried the following resolution at its Congress in Manchester, April, 1908 (to use Mr. Bax's words) "with a view to election expediency":

"That in view of the efforts of enemies of Socialism to create division and prejudice in the ranks of the workers by raising sectarian disputes, this conference definitely re-affirms the position always maintained by the International Social Democracy, that the Socialist movement is concerned solely with secular affairs and regards religion as a private matter".

It is worth noting that when the above resolution was passed, one of the S.D.P. candidates, Mr. Dan Irving, was contesting a Manchester constituency against Mr Winston Churchill. A member of the S.D.P. in that constituency, however, was selling a pamphlet entitled "Christ, the Enemy of the Human Race." The S.D.P. could not allow bourgeois respectability to be shocked with impunity; moreover, it might mean a loss of votes to the S.D.P. candidate. Hence the above resolution was passed, and the member guilty of selling an anti-Christian pamphlet was sacrificed on the altar of political expediency, and bourgeois respectability. by being expelled the organization.

Here are some more samples of "election expediency."

At the Kirkdale bye-election, 1907, Mr Hill, the Labour candidate, had the following item on his election address:

"As a Nonconformist, I believe in simple Bible study – the Bible is still my best book."

Mr. Keir Hardie, in his election address to the constituents of Merthyr Boroughs at the 1900 Parliamentary, election, said:

"My Cause is Labour's Cause, the Cause of Humanity – the Cause of God.

"I first learned my Socialisin in the New Testament, where I still find my chief inspiration".

This may explain some of the vagaries of Mr Hardie. It certainly shows that his creed, whatever else it may, be, is not Socialism.

It will be observed that application of the Socialist touchstone to the religious attitude of the so-called Labour and Social-Democratic politicians reveals the dross. Nothing is more typically small-capitalist than Nonconformity, and the servile truckling to that section of the exploiting class that is characteristic of Labour members is eloquent of their worthlessness to the toilers. Prominent Labour M.P.'s are the idols of P.S.A. Brotherhoods, and the mere fact that their "principles" are acceptable to large sections of Nonconformity is proof of their incompatibility with working class interests rightly understood.

The religious appeal, indeed, betrays the political mountebank. To attempt to obtain electoral support by the display of decomposing religious sentiment is to play the game of the enemy and to batten on ignorance. Those whose standpoint is the welfare of the working class can make no appeal on grounds of religion; for religion is an instrument of domination which cannot be used as an agent of emancipation at this stage of social development. The great theoretic weapon of the wage-workers in their fight for freedom is science, not religion, and religion and science are as incompatible as fire and water.

12 – SOCIALISTS AND THE RELIGIOUS CONFLICT

It may be urged with regard to the struggle against religion that since Socialists look upon religious ideas as shadows of society, they should not drop the substance for the shadow, but should ignore religion entirely. This, however, is incorrect, for, apart from the necessity of frankly, facing every implication of Socialism, there yet remains the fact already noted, that ideas, religious or other, have an important reflex action on society that cannot be ignored. Moreover, as Marx has put it:

"Religion is the opium of the people. The suppression of religion as the happiness of the people is the revindication of its real happiness. The invitation to abandon illusions regarding its situation is an invitation to abandon a situation which has need of illusions. Criticism of religion is therefore the germ of a criticism of the vale of tears, of which religion is the holy aspect."

Not only, indeed, is the struggle against religion intellectually useful, but it cannot conscientiously be avoided, for religion is used against the Socialist movement by the possessing class in every country. But to abolish religion is not to abolish exploitation, because only one of the enemy's guns will have been silenced. The workers have, above all, to dislodge the capitalist class from power, and the religious question, and indeed all else, is secondary to this. To say this is not to belittle the specifically anti-religious fight, but to indicate its rightful place in the greater struggle – the battle for emancipation requiring the intelligent cooperation of the great mass of the working class. Hence the test of admission to the Socialist

Party must be neither more nor less than acceptance of the essential working principles and policy of Socialism as a class movement. To demand more is to degenerate into a sect; to require less is to invite anarchy and embark on the slippery. incline of Labourisin and compromise.

These essentials of Socialist principles and policy. are outlined in the Declaration of Principles's of the Socialist Party. These can be easily understood by the average worker, and they comprise the irreducible minima of the principles and policy of Socialism; narrow enough to exclude all who are not Socialists, yet broad enough to embrace every one who is. They form, in consequence, a reasonable and sufficient test, while their acceptance logically leads to the attitude towards religion that has been outlined in these pages. If a man supports the Church, or in any respect allows religion ideas to stand in the way of the principles of Socialism or the activity of the Party, he proves thereby that he does not accept Socialism as fundamentally true and of the first importance, and his place is outside. No man can be consistently both a Socialist and a Christian. It must be either the Socialist or the religious principle that is supreme, for the attempt to couple them equally betrays charlatanism or lack of thought. There is, therefore, no need for a specifically anti-religious test. So surely does the acceptance of Socialism lead to the exclusion of the supernatural, that the Socialist has little need for such terms as atheist, Free-thinker, or even Materialist; for the word Socialist, rightly understood, implies one who on all such questions takes his stand on positive science, explaining all things by purely natural causation; Socialism being not merely a politico-economic creed, but also an integral part of a consistent world philosophy,.

13 – THE OUTLOOK

If the foregoing indication of the main stream of religious development, and of the relationship of socialist philosophy thereto, have carried with it the assent of the reader, he will agree that religion was neither the invention of priests nor a revelation from a god, but had a secular origin in savage fear and inexperience. It was the emotional reflex of primitive social life, and its successive modifications have been the results of material change. In gentile or tribal society, religion had a useful role; it helped to strengthen social bonds and gave greater cohesion to the groups of kindred. But with the disruption of patriarchal institutions its role became political; it became an instrument of class domination. Throughout political history it has served as a powerful weapon of tyranny and as the anaesthetic of the oppressed It now crumbles tardily away, in spite of the frantic efforts of the priestly cult at adaptation or restoration, and its waning influence is due to that growth of knowledge and the development of natural science, which have been made possible by economic evolution.

Under all its multifarious forms the modern mission of religion is to cloak the hideousness and injustice of social conditions and keep the exploited meek and submissive. But Socialism is the possibility of social conditions that are rational and humane and need no mask. Therefore to tear the veil of hypocrisy and mysticism from modern society is to urge the workers to end its misery and inequality. Nevertheless, the importance of the religious question must not be overestimated; it is important. but yet secondary to the great economic and political movement itself, for the supreme aim of the workers must be their emancipation from wage-slavery, and the war on superstition is but a phase of this great struggle. But it must never be forgotten that since religion is ever used as a weapon by, the ruling class against the wealth producers, no working man in the struggle for the emancipation of his class can honestly avoid the religious conflict. Our question is therefore answered. Socialism, both as a philosophy, and as a form of society, is the antithesis of religion.

The decay of religion is, indeed, a measure of the advance of humanity, for the height of man's superstition is at the same time the depth of his ignorance. The Socialist can see, accompanying the decline of religion, the toiling multitudes emerging from the darkness of ignorance and fear into the clear daylight of science and power, spurning the priests who had duped them, dispossessing the class that had robbed them, moulding society to their needs, and ordering and perfecting the social forces they have inherited. He can picture the people, no longer slaves, but free: no longer in fear of phantoms of their own creation, but looking proudly out upon a harmonious and rational social world, harnessing giant natural forces to industry, and increasing their mastery over Nature by a wider knowledge of her constant laws. He sees, moreover a social organization adapted to give all mankind health and happiness by freeing them from wasteful drudgery and by stimulating healthy emulation in a new birth of science and the arts. And so the brotherhood of man, that Christianity professed but could only retard, becomes at last a reality through the complete harmony of interests brought about by the cooperative commonweal, a brotherhood made inevitable, because the social organization makes the highest welfare and happiness of each immediately dependent upon, and producible only by the promotion of the like well-being of all.

• Further reading – Socialist Classics

Unit 1 – Short introductory works

1. The Communist Manifesto (1848) Karl Marx and Friedrich Engels

2. Wage-labour and capital (1847) Karl Marx

3. Value, Price and Profit (1865) Karl Marx

4. Socialism: Utopian and Scientific (1880) Friedrich Engels

5. The German Ideology (1846) Karl Marx and Friedrich Engels

6. Anarchism and Socialism (1895) Georgi Plekhanov

7. No Compromise, No Political Trading (1899) Wilhelm Liebknecht

8. Reform or Revolution (1900) Rosa Luxemburg

9. Leninism or Marxism? (1904) Rosa Luxemburg

10. Socialism Made Easy (1909) James Connolly

www.ingramcontent.com/pod-product-compliance
Lightning Source LLC
Chambersburg PA
CBHW070348300526
45791CB00023B/1192